COVERT CAREERS
Jobs You Can't Talk About

INSIDE THE
FBI

LOUISE SPILSBURY

LUCENT
P R E S S

Published in 2019 by
Lucent Press, an Imprint of Greenhaven Publishing, LLC
353 3rd Avenue
Suite 255
New York, NY 10010

Produced for Lucent by Calcium
Designers: Paul Myerscough and Jeni Child
Picture researcher: Rachel Blount
Editors: Sarah Eason and Jennifer Sanderson

Picture credits: Cover: Shutterstock: Photographee.eu; Inside: Federal Bureau of Investigation:
pp. 3, 5, 10, 11, 12, 15, 19, 20, 22, 24, 26, 27, 30, 32–33, 36, 37, 40, 41, 42, 43, 44; Shutterstock:
Aerogondo2: p. 16; Christian Arthur: p. 18; Gualtiero Boffi: p. 25; Lurii Chornysh: p. 23; Everett
Historical: p. 28; GaudiLab: p. 17; Anan Kaewkhammul: p. 14; Dmitry Kalinovsky: p. 39; Peter
Kim: p. 9; Phase4Studios: p. 34; Leon Rafael: p. 13; Wavebreakmedia: p. 35; Wikimedia Commons:
p. 6; Aude: p. 4; Andrea Booher/FEMA: p. 33r; Federal Bureau of Investigation: pp. 8, 21; Former
U.S. President Richard M. Nixon, officially a work of the U.S. government: p. 31; Pach Brothers: p. 7;
Robfergusonjr: p. 29; Sanders: p. 38.

Cataloging-in-Publication Data

Names: Spilsbury, Louise.
Title: Inside the FBI / Louise Spilsbury.
Description: New York : Lucent Press, 2019. | Series: Covert careers: jobs you can't talk about |
Includes glossary and index.
Identifiers: ISBN 9781534566231 (pbk.) | ISBN 9781534566248 (library bound) |
ISBN 9781534566255 (ebook)
Subjects: LCSH: United States. Federal Bureau of Investigation--Juvenile literature. |
Criminal investigation--United States--Juvenile literature. | Intelligence service--United States--
Juvenile literature. | National security--United States--Juvenile literature.
Classification: LCC HV8144.F43 S65 2019 | DDC 363.250973--dc23

Printed in the United States of America

CPSIA compliance information: Batch BW19KL: For further information, contact Greenhaven
Publishing, LLC, New York, New York, at 1-844-317-7404.

Please visit our website, www.greenhavenpublishing.com. For a free color catalog of all our
high-quality books, call toll free 1-844-317-7404 or fax 1-844-317-7405.

CONTENTS

WHAT IS THE FBI?

The FBI is an important law enforcement agency that works for the U.S. government. Its mission is to protect the people of the United States and to uphold the country's Constitution.

The Work of the FBI

FBI is an acronym for Federal Bureau of Investigation. The word "federal" refers to the national government of the United States. "Bureau" is another word for department, or division, of government. "Investigation" is what the FBI does—it gathers facts and evidence to solve and prevent crimes. In its early years, the FBI only investigated crimes such as kidnapping, bank robbery, and car theft, and it chased fugitives. Today, the FBI investigates more than 350 different kinds of crime, including terrorism, cybercrime, public corruption, spying, civil rights abuses, organized crime, and violent crime.

The public can visit the FBI Headquarters in Washington, D.C., to take a tour and see how hard the Bureau works to protect the nation.

Home of the FBI

The headquarters of the FBI is in the J. Edgar Hoover Building in Washington, D.C. This huge, bunker-like building opened in 1974, and it houses the director (the head of the FBI), most department heads, and the FBI Crime Lab. The team at FBI Headquarters supports 56 field offices in large cities and hundreds of smaller offices across the United States and in other countries, too. The regional offices around the United States support local law enforcement officers.

FBI Agents

The public face of the FBI is its agents. FBI agents have the power to make arrests and to build cases that can put suspects behind bars. Special agents have to go through an intense training program. They have to be prepared to carry out the FBI's complex mission of protecting the nation from major national security and criminal threats.

Inside the FBI

Joining the FBI is challenging—just making it to the training academy alone demands perseverance. Applicants must compete against tens of thousands of people in a grueling selection process. There are many parts to the application process, including several rounds of interviews and a thorough background check.

FBI agents must have the knowledge, skills, and commitment needed to investigate criminals.

The FBI was set up in 1908. One reason that the FBI started in 1908 was that, at that time, the world of crime was changing. There were fewer types of crime than there are today, but crime was on the rise. Cities had become bigger than ever, with increasing numbers of people crowded into them, some of whom were poor and desperate. Gangsters started to operate in the cities. There was also an increase in the production and purchase of automobiles. More cars meant more theft. People stole cars, but it also meant that criminals could escape the law more easily and move around the country on crime sprees. A lot of corrupt officials in business and industries were also breaking the law.

The Model T Ford, launched in Detroit in 1908, was the first affordable automobile and one that many people blamed for an increase in crime.

How the FBI Started

After President Roosevelt came to power, he made Charles Bonaparte the attorney general. At that time, the Justice Department relied on detectives from the Secret Service and, for a while, private detectives to help it investigate crimes. As Roosevelt cracked down on crime and introduced new laws, the Department's workload increased even more. Bonaparte decided that to tackle the rising tide of crime and corruption, he needed a squad of investigators of his own. Soon, he had persuaded Congress to allow him to employ a permanent detective force of his own. On July 26, 1908, Bonaparte brought together 34 investigators into a special agent force, and the FBI was born.

The Mystery of the Changing Name

When the FBI was started, it did not have a name. Since then, it has changed names three times. In 1909, the organization became known as the Bureau of Investigation. In 1933, the name changed to the Division of Investigation. Finally, in 1935, the FBI was given the name that stuck: the Federal Bureau of Investigation. The FBI has grown from a group of 40 to a network of more than 35,000 employees.

The FBI originated from a force of Special Agents created during the presidency of Theodore Roosevelt.

The initials "FBI" also represent the three things that the Bureau and its representatives stand for, and form its famous motto: "Fidelity—Bravery—Integrity." Fidelity means being faithful to your duty and country. Bravery means being willing to face danger, pain, or trouble. Integrity means honest and sincere, doing the right thing and making choices that are fair and just.

The FBI Seal

The Seal of the Federal Bureau of Investigation is used to represent the organization and to authenticate documents that it issues. Each symbol and color in the FBI seal has special significance:

- The color blue and the scales represent justice.
- The circle of 13 stars shows that the original 13 states were united in the same purpose.
- The 46 leaves in the two branches represent the 46 states in the Union when the FBI was founded in 1908, and the laurel leaves themselves symbolize academic honors, distinction, and fame.
- The gold in the seal conveys its importance.
- The red in the stripes stands for courage, valor, and strength, while the white symbolizes cleanliness, light, truth, and peace. As in the flag of the United States, the red bars exceed the white by one.
- The peaked edging of the seal stands for the severe challenges the FBI faces and the ruggedness of the organization.

This design for the FBI seal has been the Bureau's symbol ever since 1940.

A Badge of Honor

FBI agents carry badges with unique numbers to identify themselves and prove who they are to people when they are working on an investigation. They carry this badge in a special wallet that includes their name, an identity photograph, and credentials. FBI agents never hand someone their badge to prove who they are. They hold it up so people can see it, but they never risk letting it go.

Inside the FBI

FBI agents must be prepared to live up to the agency motto. They have to give 100 percent to their job. However, being brave does not mean rushing into danger unafraid. It means calmly and thoughtfully facing down criminals who want to do harm and bringing those criminals to justice.

FBI agents carry a badge and a set of credentials in a small case that folds in half for carrying in their pocket.

CHAPTER 2

THE FBI IN ACTION

FBI agents investigate a vast range of different crimes and threats, locally, regionally, nationally, and internationally. Their number-one priority is to protect the United States from terrorist attacks.

Terrorism

Terrorism is the unlawful use of violence and intimidation, especially against civilians, in the pursuit of political or ideological aims. Some terrorism is caused by international groups, such as Al-Qaeda, which has bombed targets in multiple countries. Other terrorist acts are carried out by violent extremists within the country. Some of the most critical terrorist threats are weapons of mass destruction (WMD). These are materials or devices intended to cause mass death or injury, for example, by exposure to poisonous and dangerous chemical substances.

Response units may locate and preserve evidence of terrorist bomb-making ingredients that can help put terrorists behind bars.

Terrorism Task Forces

The FBI collaborates with local and state law enforcement agencies in teams called task forces. It provides specialist, highly trained expertise. Terrorism Task Forces (TTFs) work to locate, disable, and disarm groups of terrorists. They foil plots, cut off sources of money paying for terrorist activities, and find evidence and seek the culprits after terrorist attacks. Some agents work in specialist teams in these TTFs.

Specialist FBI Teams:
- ✔ Evidence Response Units: tasked with finding and preserving evidence.
- ✔ FBI Dive Teams: trained and equipped to go underwater, even in contaminated lakes and rivers, to find evidence.
- ✔ Bomb Technicians: use tools, including robots, to identify, diagnose, and disrupt explosive devices. They wear suits that can protect them if a bomb detonates up close.

Dive teams investigate underwater crime scenes, sometimes in difficult conditions where visibility is low.

Tackling Terrorism

The Internet and social media are making it easier for terrorists to recruit supporters and to covertly plan and organize attacks. Trained FBI agents from the Operational Technology Division listen in on the online chatter to determine whether threats are real or hoaxes.

Inside the FBI

Being an FBI special agent is definitely not a 9-to-5 career. Special agents are always on call to protect their country from terrorism and may be transferred to different locations at any time, based on the level of threat and the needs of task forces.

Violent Crime

The FBI's focus on keeping the United States secure from terrorism does not keep it from playing an important role in combatting violent crime. Violent crimes include significant events like mass shootings, such as the October 2017 Las Vegas atrocity, and serial killings, which can stretch the resources of local and state law enforcement groups. FBI agents also help investigate and respond to other violent crimes, such as battles between street gangs, bank robberies, kidnappings, and assaults on federal officials.

FBI SWAT teams in the 56 FBI field offices are always ready to take the battle to the criminals. SWAT stands for Special Weapons and Tactics, and SWAT agents are highly mobile, fit, assault troops. They carry high-powered weaponry and wear cutting-edge protective suits. Some are specialist snipers. Snipers are shooters who can shoot accurately at a distance to injure or kill.

SWAT can move into action at a moment's notice, in the area, around the country, or elsewhere in the world.

This is a selection of firearms seized by FBI agents during the course of their investigations.

Crime Without Borders

Transnational Organized Crime (TOC) groups are criminal gangs that operate across borders. They become rich or powerful in many ways. Some specialize, for example, in importing and exporting illegal drugs or firearms, or endangered animals and plants. Some produce counterfeit medicines and money to trade for profit, while others run illegal gambling rings. TOC groups typically use violence and corruption to protect their activities, such as threatening and bribing customs officials to let shipments past. The goal of the FBI and its agents is to bring down entire TOCs, not just to arrest select individuals. This can require dangerous undercover work to infiltrate gangs and find out what they are doing.

Inside the FBI

An agent's daily tasks vary, from arresting suspects and testifying in court, to searching a crime scene for evidence or gathering intelligence from documents or computers. That is why adaptability and a willingness to learn and take on different roles are important skills for trainee FBI agents.

13

Human Trafficking

Human trafficking is the buying, selling, and smuggling of people. Victims can be beaten, starved, threatened, drugged, and forced to work for little or no pay in places such as factories, farms, and construction sites. They may be moved from one country to another, but a lot of human trafficking in the United States involves U.S. citizens who are shifted from state to state.

The FBI works on human trafficking cases as part of both its Civil Rights program and its Violent Crimes Against Children program. The priority is to rescue the victims. Agents work with other organizations to help rescued victims with support, such as shelter and clothing, and to set up education and counseling. The human trafficking program amasses evidence, often using undercover agents and surveillance wires, to help break up trafficking rings.

Every year, many thousands of men, women, and children fall into the hands of traffickers in their own countries and overseas.

Cybercrime

Most people use computer or cellular Internet to shop, bank, store data, and operate devices. It is no surprise that criminals are on the rampage in cyberspace, using various fraud schemes to steal money, hacking websites to get personal data to sell, and disrupting businesses. Some operate as part of large TOCs or terrorist organizations, but others work for foreign powers seeking to steal government and military secrets. The FBI Cyber Division has specially trained cyber squads that investigate computer intrusions, theft, and fraud. They are IT experts who can crack codes, read programs, and follow the trail of cybercrumbs leading back to criminals. Cyber Action teams are always prepared to travel globally to gather intelligence that may prevent large cybercrimes.

Ransomware

Ransomware is software distributed by email that locks up data on someone's computer and demands a ransom to make the data available again. This cybercrime is on the increase. In 2017, more than 100,000 organizations in 150 countries were affected by one type of ransomware. Fortunately, a computer expert found a solution, so few people lost money. However, targets included hospitals, school districts, state and local governments, and law enforcement agencies that have important data.

Agents with special training in cybercrime at FBI headquarters and in the 56 field offices use state-of-the-art technology to tackle this growing problem.

THE FBI TEAM

At the FBI, there is a wide variety of career paths available for individuals from all backgrounds and experiences. To help the agents investigate and bring a case against criminals, there is a huge support team at the FBI that works in an exciting variety of different specialized roles.

Language Specialists

Language specialists are fluent in different languages. They use their knowledge of other languages and cultures to help the FBI in several ways. They can translate something from another language, such as Japanese, Korean, or German, into English to tell FBI agents what a document means. They may also be called on to translate what a suspect says when FBI agents are interviewing them.

FBI language specialists get the opportunity to travel widely for specific cases.

Forensic Accountants

An FBI forensic accountant studies bank accounts and financial documents to look for suspicious irregularities. The accountants then link these funding sources to criminal activity and national security matters. They also provide reports to support their findings. Their reports may offer reconstructions and insights into how the activities were carried out. They may also uncover potential new leads to help special agents catch a criminal or criminal organization. Forensic accountants must have:

✔ Meticulous attention to detail
✔ Excellent numeracy skills
✔ The mind-set of a detective

Legal and
Administration Roles

There are a lot of people who work to make sure the FBI runs smoothly, from those who design FBI field offices to those who maintain the fleets of cars and the computers the FBI relies on. The FBI employs healthcare professionals who assess and treat routine and emergency healthcare needs of the workforce. FBI police and security professionals work together to keep FBI employees safe. There are lawyers and legal workers who advise the FBI on international and domestic law enforcement and intelligence investigations, and help the FBI take their cases to court.

Administrative staff supports agents in their work and are the backbone of the organization.

Scientists in Action

Some members of the support team are scientists who work in an office or in a laboratory, where they examine evidence. There are many kinds of scientists who work at the FBI:

- Some scientists study hair, bones, or skin to help them identify a body. For example, they can tell how old someone is by looking at the bones in a skeleton.
- Some scientists look at paint chips left on a wall by a car or other vehicle, then figure out how many times and what different colors a car has been painted.
- Cryptanalysts are able break secret codes that a spy or criminal uses on their computer to hide important information.

Entomologists

Entomologists study insects to help solve a crime. This often means using insects to estimate the time since a victim died. Once a person dies, their body starts to rot, a process that is helped along by insects. It is by collecting and studying the insects that are feeding on a body that a forensic entomologist can estimate the time elapsed since the person died. For example, flies rapidly discover and lay eggs on bodies, usually ahead of beetles.

FBI scientists, such as entomologists, study evidence collected from the site of criminal investigations.

The Writing Is on the Wall

Other members of the support team include fingerprint experts who can identify a person by the fingerprints they leave behind at a scene. Handwriting analysts are also known as graphologists. They study the characteristics and patterns of a person's handwriting to try to identify the writer's personality traits and how they were feeling at the time of writing.

Inside the FBI

FBI scientists usually have a degree in forensic science. This helps them get an entry-level position as a lab analyst or crime scene or fingerprint technician. During their degree course, they study subjects such as biology, general chemistry, analytical chemistry, anatomy, criminal justice, anthropology, and psychology.

Evidence response teams are specially trained to collect evidence to be investigated in the lab in such a way that does not damage it.

Intelligence analysts help gather, share, and make sense of information and intelligence about subjects and suspected crimes from around the world. Intelligence analysts study the information, so that they can tell special agents and others what they think it means and how it can be used to combat threats and convict criminals. They also work to identify attacks before they occur and analyze information for agents in the field. Intelligence Analysts also have to make snap judgments and decisions about how agents should act on information.

Profilers

FBI profilers work for the Bureau's Behavioral Analysis Unit (BAU). They look at evidence and circumstances surrounding a crime or series of crimes, and create a profile of a suspect. A profile is a description of what the suspect or suspects might be like, including their gender, age, standard of education, and what type of work they might do. This helps agents narrow down a list of suspects in an investigation. The FBI also employs geographical profilers. They feed information about the locations of crimes into a computer, and they use programs to define an area of interest where investigators can focus their efforts.

Profilers analyze crime photos, evidence, and witness reports to help them create a criminal profile.

Surveillance Specialists

Special Surveillance Group members are also known as Investigative Specialists, or even "ghosts," because of their ability to gather intelligence without being seen. Fixed surveillance workers gather intelligence in an office or indoor setting using technical equipment. Mobile surveillance groups work on the move, following subjects on foot, in a vehicle, or on public transportation. They carry outfits in their cars that help them blend in with a crowd in different situations. Some even travel with a bicycle in their trunk, so that they can ride through the streets pretending to be messengers.

Surveillance Specialists do not have to go through the FBI's rigorous training program to become Special Agents. However, they do need to be able to:

✔ Blend in with a crowd
✔ Work in a team
✔ Work nights and weekends when necessary
✔ Adapt to an ever-changing work environment
✔ Work with photography and other electronic equipment

Surveillance missions can be monitored from a mobile command center like this one.

CHAPTER 4

TECHNIQUES AND TOOLS

FBI officers use many different kinds of techniques and tools to help them solve crimes and make a case watertight, so that the criminal will be convicted.

Fingerprint Analysis

Fingerprints are the perfect way to link a criminal to a crime because everyone's fingerprints are unique. Hair color and other features can alter over time, and people can dye their hair and put on spectacles to change the way they look. However, their fingerprints never change. The FBI has fingerprint records for more than 100 million people, and it receives thousands of new ones every day. Using new technology, officers sift through these records to find a match quickly.

Some fingerprints are easy to see, but the FBI is also able to detect latent fingerprints: those that are invisible to the naked eye.

In a polygraph test, equipment such as finger plates are attached to two of the subject's fingers.

Polygraph Tests

FBI agents also have a machine that can tell if a person is telling the truth or lying when they answer questions in an interview. This machine is called a polygraph, but it is more commonly known as a lie detector. A polygraph works by sensing and measuring how the person's body reacts when they are asked a question. First, the FBI interviewer asks simple questions that can be answered only with a "yes" or a "no," such as, "Are you 50 years old?" and then more complicated questions, such as, "Have you ever lied to someone who trusts you?" The machine measures the suspect's blood pressure, their pulse (the number of times a minute their heart beats), the amount they sweat, and the rate at which they respire, or breathe. By analyzing the results, the FBI examiner can judge whether or not the suspect is telling the truth.

Forensic Lights

In the past, the conventional method for gathering prints was to first dust black powder on them, then lift the powder onto a sticky sheet. Today, agents in the field use a forensic light source, which uses different types of light to spot previously invisible prints or those that are too difficult to lift. This increases the types of surfaces from which a fingerprint can be detected, such as thin plastic bags or heavily grained wood.

Surveillance Equipment

FBI surveillance officers use a variety of tools to gather intelligence to help them identify domestic and international threats. Sometimes, they will use cameras to secretly photograph cars, suspects, and places in which they think a crime may have been committed. They also set up surveillance cameras that record and relay activities on a street. Sometimes, the cameras are attached to utility poles. Officers can also hide microphones in public places to listen to criminals speaking to each other in a place where they think no one can hear them.

The surveillance of an area, building, or person—often from a stationary vehicle—is called a stakeout.

Wiretapping

When a listening device is connected to a telephone line or cell phone signal to monitor conversations, it is called wiretapping. The wire is attached secretly and is kept concealed, so that the people using the telephone or cell phone do not know that their conversations are being monitored. Wiretapping is strictly controlled by federal law and is mostly used to combat terrorism and the most serious crimes.

Surveillance teams may also plant a "bug" inside private property to secretly record conversations. Electronic surveillance can tell the FBI who is involved in a crime or criminal organization, as well as what that organization is doing and where. The recordings made of conversations or meetings can also be used in court to help prosecute criminals.

Working in FBI surveillance teams requires certain characteristics:

The FBI also rents rooms or offices near a suspect to carry out surveillance. Stakeouts like this may last for weeks or months.

✔ Fitness: Members must have 20/20 corrected vision in one eye and no less than 20/40 in the other eye. They must pass a color vision test and a hearing examination.

✔ Patience: People may be assigned to cases that last for months and have to remain attentive during periods when nothing happens.

✔ Observant: They must be on watch for anything and everything, noting even the smallest changes.

✔ Precise: Team members have to keep careful records of even a target's most boring activities, in case it proves useful later on in the investigation.

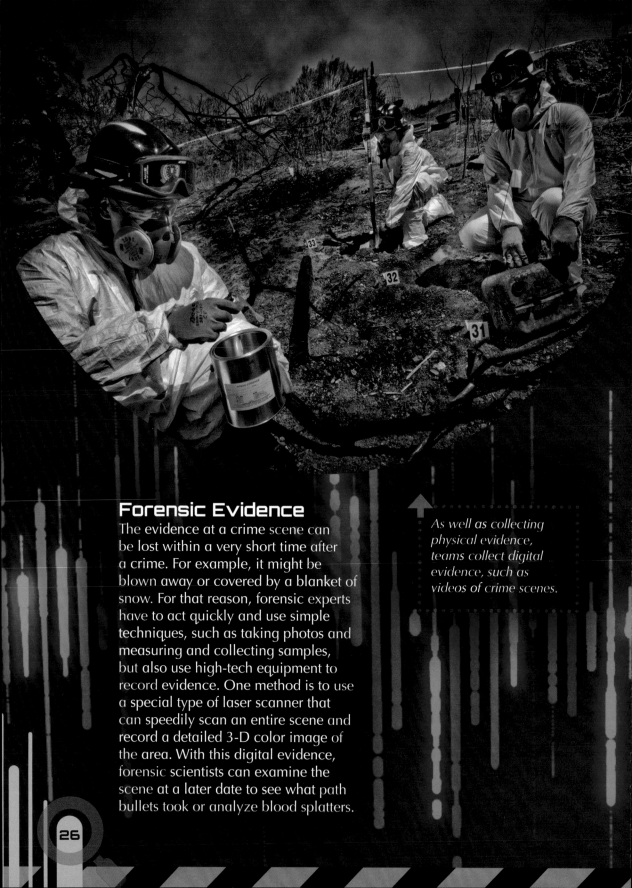

Forensic Evidence

The evidence at a crime scene can be lost within a very short time after a crime. For example, it might be blown away or covered by a blanket of snow. For that reason, forensic experts have to act quickly and use simple techniques, such as taking photos and measuring and collecting samples, but also use high-tech equipment to record evidence. One method is to use a special type of laser scanner that can speedily scan an entire scene and record a detailed 3-D color image of the area. With this digital evidence, forensic scientists can examine the scene at a later date to see what path bullets took or analyze blood splatters.

As well as collecting physical evidence, teams collect digital evidence, such as videos of crime scenes.

DNA Analysis

If there are no fingerprints at a crime scene or the fingerprints found do not match any of those on record, another way of linking a criminal to a crime is using DNA analysis. The human body is made up of millions of tiny building blocks called cells, which are too small to see with the naked eye. Inside each of these cells are even smaller parts called DNA. DNA is like the blueprint for the way each person develops. It is a unique code that determines what they look like, how tall they are, what color eyes they have, and so on. Every cell in a person's body—from heart to skin, blood to bones—contains a complete set of their DNA. Forensic scientists can run a sample taken from a suspect through a special machine and then look for similarities in the genetic markers between it and DNA found at a crime scene.

Catching a Killer

The first American to be convicted using DNA evidence was serial killer Timothy Wilson Spencer. David Vasquez, who had been wrongly convicted of one of Spencer's crimes before Spencer was caught, was the first man in the United States to be cleared by DNA testing.

Scientists can extract DNA from a variety of sources, including skin cells, blood, a single hair, and sweat.

CHAPTER 5

FAMOUS FBI CASES

The FBI's important work is ongoing and often happens in the background. However, through its history, the FBI has been involved in some very famous investigations of a wide range of crimes.

The Lindbergh Kidnapping

Charles Lindbergh was an aviator who became famous after becoming the first person to fly nonstop across the Atlantic in 1927. His achievement earned him a $25,000 prize.

On March 1, 1932, Lindbergh's 20-month-old son was kidnapped from his home. A handwritten ransom note was found on the windowsill demanding money in return for the infant's life. More ransom notes arrived, but before the Lindberghs could pay, the baby was found dead.

These are the artist's sketches of the Lindbergh baby kidnapper. These sketches helped the FBI find and arrest him.

So began one of the FBI laboratory's first cases. Special Agent Charles Appel compared the handwriting on the notes to handwriting samples from 300 suspects, with no match. Then sketches based on an eyewitness account of a man spotted near Lindbergh's house at the time of the kidnapping were matched to Bruno Hauptmann, who was arrested. Appel found a match between the notes and Hauptmann's writing. The FBI also found a match between wood fibers from a ladder the kidnapper used and wood in Hauptmann's home. As a result, Hauptmann was convicted of the kidnapping and sentenced to death.

Mississippi Burning

In the mid-1960s, the Civil Rights movement was growing in influence in the southern U.S. states. However, a far-right hate group called the Ku Klux Klan carried out campaigns of terror, in an attempt to slow the pace of change. The FBI investigated many of the Klan's atrocities, including a case named for a car burned by Klansmen who had murdered three civil rights workers in Mississippi in June 1964. The FBI arrested 18 suspects, including a preacher named Edgar Killen and a deputy sheriff. After years of court cases, seven people were found guilty of the murders—but not Killen. He was released because one jury member could not believe that a preacher could be guilty. However, the FBI found further evidence over time and finally convicted Killen in 2005.

This history marker remembers the case of the Mississippi civil rights workers' murders, which were solved by the FBI.

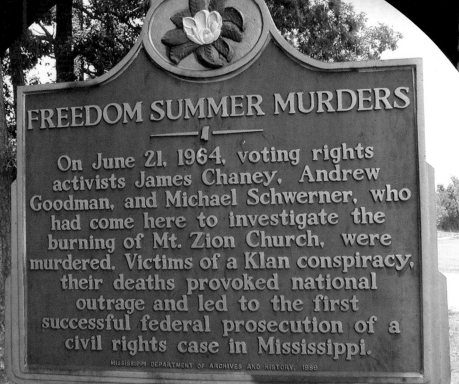

FREEDOM SUMMER MURDERS

On June 21, 1964, voting rights activists James Chaney, Andrew Goodman, and Michael Schwerner, who had come here to investigate the burning of Mt. Zion Church, were murdered. Victims of a Klan conspiracy, their deaths provoked national outrage and led to the first successful federal prosecution of a civil rights case in Mississippi.

MISSISSIPPI DEPARTMENT OF ARCHIVES AND HISTORY, 1989

Watergate

The most famous political corruption case in which the FBI was ever involved was named after a Washington, D.C., hotel complex: Watergate. This is where the Democratic National Committee's headquarters were based. On June 17, 1972, a night guard noticed an exit door from the headquarters that was suspiciously taped open, and police arrived to catch intruders in the process of fitting microphones to spy on what went on in the offices. The FBI became involved immediately when they heard one of the intruders was a member of staff of the Republican president, Richard Nixon. The staff member was involved in a political campaign to get Nixon reelected, called CRP. Nixon denied any involvement in the spying and was reelected. Several of the intruders were found guilty of trying to spy.

The Watergate complex became well known in the wake of the scandal that led to the end of Nixon's presidency.

Cover-Up

However, the FBI investigation continued. Many people, from politicians to reporters, were not convinced that Nixon was innocent and suspected an official cover-up. Over the coming months, the FBI managed to collect more evidence, even though there was enormous pressure from the government for them to stop investigating a U.S. president.

Some people believed that Nixon had ordered the spies to bug the Democrats in order to find ways to beat them in the election. His spies had previously stolen documents and tried to bug the Democrats' headquarters, but had returned on the night of their arrest because a microphone was faulty! When the FBI was closing in on Nixon, he tried to use the Central Intelligence Agency (CIA) to impede their investigation. Eventually, the FBI found enough evidence to prove that Nixon had obstructed justice and covered up criminal activity. Nixon resigned from office in August 1974.

This is President Nixon's letter of resignation, dated August 9, 1974.

THE WHITE HOUSE
WASHINGTON

August 9, 1974

Dear Mr. Secretary:

I hereby resign the Office of President of the United States.

Sincerely,

Richard Nixon

11.35 AM

The Honorable Henry A. Kissinger
The Secretary of State
Washington, D.C. 20520

HK

Self-Destructing Tape

Important evidence confirming Nixon's guilt came from tape recordings of himself. He had routinely taped all conversations in the White House, even those with his conspirators. Nixon argued it was his presidential executive privilege to not share White House recordings with the FBI, but eventually, he was forced to hand them over.

9/11 Attacks

The largest and most complex investigation the FBI has ever conducted began on the fateful morning on September 11, 2001. Two airliners crashed into the World Trade Center towers in Manhattan, New York City, causing them to collapse. Another flew into the Pentagon in Virginia and a fourth crashed in a field in rural Pennsylvania. These events killed thousands of people in the airliners and the structures they crashed into, including hundreds of emergency service workers attempting to save people from the towers. They also caused widespread destruction.

Massive Investigation

The FBI needed to use more than half of its total personnel and all of its specialist resources to investigate the crimes. For example, their Critical Incident Response Groups checked crash sites for possible explosives and hazards. Evidence Response teams started the task of recovering human remains and preserving physical evidence by sifting through millions of tons of rubble. They worked with the New York Police Department's Missing Persons Unit to identify victims and also the perpetrators of the destruction. Other FBI teams took photographs of crash scenes and established links between DNA found in the airliners and that found in hotel rooms where the hijackers stayed before the attacks. They also trawled the hijackers' computers for evidence. These statistics show the scale of the task and its findings:

Some FBI agents worked in forensic recovery operations at the sites of the 9/11 terror attacks.

9/11 Statistics:
- ✔ 2,977 deaths occurred
- ✔ 4,000 FBI special agents involved
- ✔ 7,500 pieces of evidence gathered
- ✔ 45,000 crime scene photographs taken
- ✔ 167,000 interviews with witnesses carried out
- ✔ 126,632 fingerprint comparisons made, from approximately 3,833 pieces of evidence
- ✔ 35 terabytes of data (just in the first 30 days after the crash) gathered

FBI agents teamed up with the New York Police Department after the terror attacks to identify victims and find the terrorists who caused them.

Conviction

Using the vast amount of information, the FBI helped to identify 19 hijackers who died as they crashed the airliners and who carried out the attacks on behalf of Al-Qaeda. By 2003, the FBI had established that the attack had been planned and coordinated by Zacarias Moussaoui. He was arrested and, in April 2005, pleaded guilty to his participation in the 9/11 conspiracy. In May 2006, he was sentenced to life in prison.

A COVERT CAREER

Working for the FBI as a special agent is one of the most exciting careers a person can choose. The FBI is one of the most highly held intelligence agencies in the world —so, how do people land this covert role?

Suit the Service?

Before they join the FBI, people need to first make sure that they are suited to the service. It is important that they analyze their personality carefully. The FBI searches for key traits in their people—these are characteristics that will make them a great officer. Below are some of the most important characteristics:

✔ Friendliness—Agents need to work well with others. Someone who is argumentative or is unfriendly will not win the trust of others.

✔ Problem-solving—They must be able to think quickly and on their feet.

✔ Observation skills—It is important to notice detail, so agents must blend in with groups that they are trying to infiltrate.

✔ Adaptability—Agents must be able to quickly adapt to changing situations.

FBI agents are the face of the Bureau. However, behind them is a team of skilled experts who help set up their operations, and keep them secret.

Fit for the Agency

Candidates must be superfit to take on the demanding role of FBI agent. New recruits are rigorously tested to make sure they are mentally and physically able to do the job. The FBI will not take a candidate for its selection process unless they meet rigorous physical standards.

FBI agents must stay fit, too. The test is designed to ensure that they can move quickly during a mass shooting and chase and catch suspects. So, even seasoned officers in the FBI who spend their days filing paperwork sitting behind a desk have to take fitness tests. The results are then included in their annual performance reviews.

Active fitness training is a vital part of getting and keeping a job with the FBI.

Inside the FBI

To work as an FBI agent, each candidate is tested in the following exercises, with only a 5-minute break between each activity:

- *The number of sit-ups they can do in 1 minute*
- *A timed 300-yard (275 m) sprint*
- *The number of continuous push-ups they can do*
- *A timed 1.5-mile (2.4 km) run*

Weapons Training

Guns and other weapons can be very dangerous in the wrong hands, so one of the most important things that new agents learn is how to handle their guns safely. They are taught how to clean their guns and how to shoot accurately at a target. Trainees spend hundreds of hours on the shooting range to become proficient with a variety of firearms, including the pistol, shotgun, and carbine. Even after trainees complete their training, they are required to return to a shooting range regularly to be retested on their target skills.

New agents must learn how to care for and fire their guns safely and effectively. A handling mistake could lead to injury or even death.

Vehicle Training

Trainees also have to learn safe, efficient driving techniques in order to track and catch criminals and terrorists and avoid being harmed by them. The driving skills they learn prepare agents to handle a variety of dangerous situations, such as high-speed chases and reversing out of alleyways under fire. They also learn techniques including how to ram a threatening vehicle. In the training, the instructors use real-life situation exercises that give trainees only seconds to spot danger and react.

Inside the FBI

At the FBI driving school, trainees learn and perfect driving skills on a 1.1-mile (1.7 m) oval road track. An instructor tells the trainees to weave in and out of orange traffic cones on an obstacle course. This teaches them skills such as emergency breaking, how to change lanes quickly and safely in order to avoid crashing into something, and how to dodge a bullet from a car pursuing them.

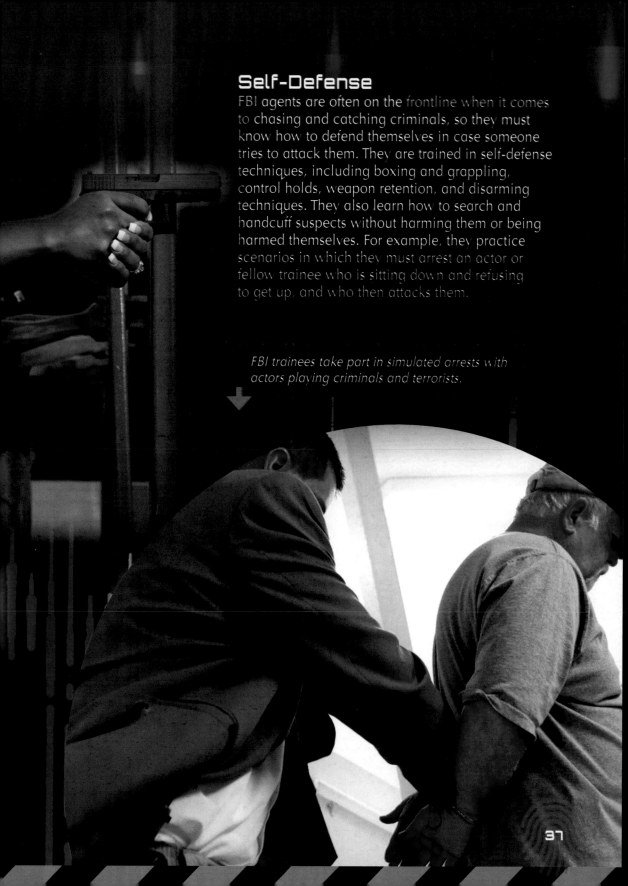

Self-Defense

FBI agents are often on the frontline when it comes to chasing and catching criminals, so they must know how to defend themselves in case someone tries to attack them. They are trained in self-defense techniques, including boxing and grappling, control holds, weapon retention, and disarming techniques. They also learn how to search and handcuff suspects without harming them or being harmed themselves. For example, they practice scenarios in which they must arrest an actor or fellow trainee who is sitting down and refusing to get up, and who then attacks them.

FBI trainees take part in simulated arrests with actors playing criminals and terrorists.

Hogan's Alley

Hogan's Alley looks and feels like a real town, but it is totally fake. In fact, it is a tactical training facility of more than 10 acres (40,000 sq m) run by the FBI Training Academy. Hogan's Alley was opened in 1987. It is used as a realistic setting for training agents of not only the FBI, but also the Drug Enforcement Agency (DEA) and other law enforcement agents.

On the Street

Hogan's Alley has many of the buildings an ordinary town would have: a bank (where there are at least five robberies a week), a post office, a hotel, a laundromat, a pool hall, homes, and stores. There are cars parked in the street and lined up with "for sale" notices. People come and go from the stores and eat in the deli. Turning up to work in the town every day are actors who role-play different characters in different scenarios. They might play innocent bystanders, terrorists, bank robbers, drug dealers, or members of criminal gangs.

WELCOME TO HOGAN'S ALLEY
CITY   LIMITS

CAUTION: LAW ENFORCEMENT TRAINING EXERCISES IN PROGRESS. DISPLAY OF WEAPONS FIRING OF BLANK AMMUNITION AND ARRESTS MAY OCCUR. IF CHALLENGED PLEASE FOLLOW INSTRUCTIONS.

HAVE A NICE DAY

This sign outside Hogan's Alley warns people that it is not a real town because it looks so realistic!

Hollywood and Hogan's Alley

Hogan's Alley was officially opened in 1987 and was built with the help of Hollywood set designers. The name was inspired by a 1890s comic strip about a New York tenement called Hogan's Alley. The alley was located in a rough neighborhood, so the FBI thought the name fit their crime-ridden town, too.

Training for Real Life

No amount of sitting in a classroom can really prepare agents for real-life events. So, in Hogan's Alley, trainees learn by actually carrying out investigations into fake terrorist activities. They learn when to shoot and not to shoot, how to make arrests and deal with criminals who resist arrest, how to process evidence at crime scenes, and much more. They also learn to use shields as protection and how to clear areas and buildings, so they are safe to enter.

At Hogan's Alley:

✔ Trainees have to use what they learned in the FBI Academy classrooms and apply it to scenarios reflecting cyber, criminal, and terrorist attacks.

✔ The scenarios put them in high-stress, challenging situations where they have to think quickly and act fast.

✔ The FBI evaluates how well the students do, and their success determines whether the or not they get to be an intelligence officer.

Realistic paintball bullets are fired from fake but realistic-looking guns in simulated gun fights, with actors playing criminals and terrorists.

In the Classroom

FBI trainees also spend a lot of time in the classroom, learning about a broad range of subjects. They have to learn rules about the law and correct legal processes that have to be followed. For example, they need to know all of the rules governing searches, or else questions could be raised during a trial about the credibility of recovered evidence. They learn about ethics, including the importance of protecting and serving with compassion and fairness, and upholding the rule of law. They are taught: interviewing, investigative, and intelligence techniques; how to collect evidence; and how to write reports. They learn how to encourage witnesses to cooperate and how to find and deal with informants, as well as how to handle physical and electronic surveillance equipment.

If trainees do not learn to follow the correct procedures, criminals can escape conviction.

Operational Skills

As well as learning to drive, shoot, and defend themselves, FBI trainee agents need to learn how to gather intelligence, conduct interviews, and dig up more clues. They learn how to do these things alongside FBI intelligence analysts, who are training to help gather, share, and make sense of information and intelligence from around the world. They learn how to identify threats and how to make judgments that are logical and well-thought-out. By training together, the FBI trainee agents and analysts experience what they need to do and how to work together, so that they are ready to do so once they have real-life cases in a field office.

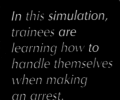

In this simulation, trainees are learning how to handle themselves when making an arrest.

Inside the FBI

As part of FBI ethics training, recruits tour the United States Holocaust Memorial Museum and learn about how the Nazis took power in Germany in 1933 with the help of civilian police. They also visit the Martin Luther King, Jr. Memorial; the FBI was wrongfully investigating Dr. King when he was assassinated. These trips are designed to remind trainees of past FBI mistakes, the importance of civil rights, and the need for accountability.

Graduation Day

After more than 800 hours in and out of the FBI classroom learning what it takes to become a special agent, trainees finally reach their goal. The new recruits have worked, studied, and sweated together to complete an incredibly challenging experience. Now, at last, they receive their FBI badge and credentials on graduation day. They walk forward onto a stage, one after the other, raise their right hands and repeat the FBI oath, after which they can walk across the stage to get their credentials and badge. The next stop is the weapons vault, where they collect their FBI-issue gun and bullets. Then, they are ready to get to work protecting lives and arresting dangerous criminals and terrorists.

It takes a great deal of studying, training, and dedication before an FBI agent can graduate.

The Training Never Stops

The pressure to learn and train continues after graduation. New agents have to report to their first field office. At first, they are on probation and are given a training mentor who will monitor their progress and help them learn on the job. For the first three years of their careers, they must reach specific targets and objectives before they are allowed to operate more independently in investigations. Even after that, FBI agents are expected to keep training. Lifelong learning is absolutely essential for an FBI agent to stay on their game and survive in the dangerous world of crime and criminals.

The FBI Oath

I (name) do solemnly swear (or affirm) that I will support and defend the Constitution of the United States against all enemies, foreign and domestic; that I will bear true faith and allegiance to the same; that I take this obligation freely, without any mental reservation or purpose of evasion; and that I will well and faithfully discharge the duties of the office on which I am about to enter. So help me God.

Every qualified agent must continually train and work hard to be an FBI agent.

A COVERT CAREER IN THE FBI

Would you like a covert career in the FBI? Following these steps will help set you on your path.

At School

You do not need to study particular subjects, but math, science, engineering, psychology, and technology will be useful. Take opportunities to practice teamwork while at school, and try to mix and deal with people from different backgrounds.

A Higher Degree

A bachelor's degree is the required minimum for employment as an FBI agent, but having a higher degree could help you stand out in the competitive application process. If you get a master's degree in a field such as criminology, this could help you to get a more specialized special agent position.

At College

To be an FBI special agent, you must have a bachelor's degree. The type of degree depends on which entry program you are interested in. Currently, five entry programs exist for special agent candidates: Computer Science and Information, Accounting, Language, Law, and Diversified. (The diversified entry program specifies that applicants hold a Bachelor of Science or Bachelor of Arts.)

Driver's License

Candidates must possess a valid U.S. driver's license.

before they will be accepted, and have to take part in regular fitness tests throughout their career.

Age Requirements

To become an agent, you must be at least 23 years old at the time of your appointment. You must also be younger than 37, unless you qualify for an age waiver available to veterans.

Work Experience

Candidates must have complete at least three years of profession work experience in their area of expertise, for example, within th police force.

Successful Applicants

You must pass a polygraph, a drug test, and an extensive background check that can take several months. Background checks into all your records are carried out and include interviews with people you have had contact with throughout your life. You will not be accepted if you have ever been convicted of any crime or have failed to pay student loans.

The Training: Once your application has been accepted, you must complete 20 weeks of on-campus training at the FBI Academy. If you pass all the tests here, you will graduate and get your FBI badge and gun.

On Probation: After graduation, you will be assigned to a field office, where you will begin a 2-year probationary period watched over by a mentor who will help you apply your training to real assignments.

Becoming an FBI Officer: After 2 years of probation, you will finally become a fully-fledged FBI special agent.

GLOSSARY

authenticate To prove or show (something) to be true, genuine, or valid.

Central Intelligence Agency (CIA) The U.S. government intelligence service that gathers and analyzes national security information about other countries from around the world.

civil rights The rights that each person has, regardless of race, sex, or religion, to freedom, justice, and equality.

conspirators People who are involved in a plan to do something illegal.

convict To find a person guilty of a crime and sentence them to a punishment.

corruption Acting dishonestly in return for money or personal gain.

counseling When a professional helps a person through their emotional or psychological problems.

counterfeit An exact copy of something valuable made with the intention to deceive or defraud.

credentials Evidence that proves a person does have the qualifications or job they say they have.

crime sprees Series of crimes committed by the same people in a short period of time.

Drug Enforcement Administration (DEA) An arm of the U.S. Department of Justice that regulates the use of drugs.

DNA The chemical code found in every cell of the human body that makes each person unique.

ethics The moral ideas that make us do the right thing.

executive privilege The privilege claimed by the president for the executive branch of the U.S. government, of withholding information in the public interest.

field offices Offices away from an organization's main office that are part of the main operation.

genetic markers DNA sequences that can be used to identify individuals.

ideological Political, cultural, or religious beliefs.

infiltrate To secretly become part of a group in order to get information.

informants People who give information to others, usually people who tell law enforcement officers about criminals.

intimidation Frightening or threatening someone, usually to persuade them to do something.

organized crime Serious crimes that are planned and controlled by powerful groups and carried out on a large scale.

perpetrators People who carry out an illegal, criminal, or evil act.

probation A period of time when a person is tested to see if they can behave in a certain way or perform certain tasks in an acceptable manner.

Secret Service A U.S. government organization responsible for keeping important people, such as the president, safe.

FOR MORE INFORMATION

BOOKS

Colich, Abby. *U.S. Federal Agents: FBI Agents*. North Mankato, MN: Capstone Press, 2018.

Larson, Kirsten W. *Protecting Our People: The FBI*. Mankato, MN: Amicus, 2016.

Mara, Wil. *21st Century Skills Library: Cool STEAM Careers: FBI Special Agent*. North Mankato, MN: Cherry Lake Publishing, 2015.

Mitchell, Megan. *My Government: Standing in the FBI Director's Shoes*. New York, NY: Cavendish Square, 2018.

Yasuda, Anita. *Girls in Science: Forensics: Cool Women Who Investigate*. White River Junction, VT: Nomad Press, 2016.

WEBSITES

Find out more about how the FBI works at:
people.howstuffworks.com/fbi.htm

Go on a mission with the FBI at:
archives.fbi.gov/archives/fun-games/kids

Read more about the FBI training academy at:
www.fbi.gov/services/training-academy

Learn more about how to become an agent at:
study.com/articles/How_to_Become_a_FBI_Special_Agent.html

Discover all the jobs that are available at the FBI at:
www.fbijobs.gov/career-paths

INDEX